Liechtenstein Travel Guide.

Tourism

Author
Jesse Russell

Publisher:
SONITTEC LTD
College House, 2nd
Floor
17 King Edwards
Road,
Ruislip
London
HA4 7AE .

Table of Content

Summary 1
Liechtenstein Introduction 10
About Liechtenstein 13
Guide to Liechtenstein...............................13
Soul of Liechtenstein 19
Languages & religions 19
Useful info...24
Best transportation means....................24
When to visit climate 29
Political life 35
Economics and GDP 40
The History..46
Refoundation of Liechtenstein 48
20th century 50
The People 54
Population 54
Demography 54
Languages 56
Religions 58
Healthcare system 60
Welfare system...................................62
Family policy.......................................64
Clubs and societies..............................67
Geography 69
Location...69
Climate 71
Flora 75
Fauna 78
Geology and mountains 80
Lakes and rivers 82
Culture...85
Culture policy.......................................85
Traditions 87

Customs.. 88

Special traditions 90

Legends 93

Food and drink... 96

Theatre and dance... 98

Music 101

Josef Gabriel Rheinberger 101

Liechtenstein Music School 103

From brass bands to the blues................................. 106

Art.. 108

Art scene 108

Liechtenstein Cultural Foundation........................... 110

Museums and exhibitions 111

Triesen... 115

Summary

How Traveling Can Broaden Your Perspective
Liechtenstein Tourism: You may not need a lot of convincing when it comes to finding a reason to travel especially when considering a trip to a foreign country. Exploring the world, seeing new places, and learning about new cultures are just a few of the benefits of traveling. There is value to exploring someplace new and combating the stress of getting out of your comfort zone.

Traveling should be looked at as a journey for personal growth, mental health, and spiritual enlightenment. Taking the time to travel to a new place can both literally and figuratively open your eyes to things you have never seen before. These new experiences allow you to get to know yourself in ways you can't if you stay in the same place.

- ✓ Traveling is wonderful in so many ways:
- ✓ You can indulge your sense of wanderlust.
- ✓ You experience different cultures.
- ✓ Your taste buds get to experience unique foods.
- ✓ You meet all different kinds of people.

As you grow older, your mind evolves and expands to adapt to the new information you receive. Traveling to a new destination is similar in this way, but the learning process occurs at a faster rate. Traveling thrusts you into the unknown and delivers you with a bounty of new information and ideas. The expansion of your mind is one of the greatest benefits of travel. Keep reading to learn six more benefits of traveling.

> Discover Your Purpose: Feeling as though you have a purpose in life is more important than many people realize. A purpose connects you to something bigger than yourself and keeps you moving forward. Your purpose in life can change suddenly and fluidly as you enter new stages in becoming who you are. With each new stage in life, there comes new goals and callings. Traveling can help open your eyes to a new life direction. You may be wandering down a path unaware of where you will end up. Seeing new places and meeting new people can help you break from that path and discover what your true purpose is.

Traveling is an excellent remedy for when you feel you need to refocus on your purpose and goals, or re-evaluate your life path. There is no better time to open your eyes than when your life seems to be out of focus and in need of redirection. You might just be surprised by what you discover and find a new sense of life purpose how traveling changes you.

Traveling is a way to discover parts of yourself that you never knew existed. While traveling, you have no choice but to deal with unexpected situations. For example, how you may typically handle a problem at home might be a completely unacceptable approach when you are in an unfamiliar place without all of the comforts and conveniences of home.

> Be Aware of Your Blessings: When you travel to a new destination, your eyes are opened to new standards, and, you become more aware of all the blessings and privileges you have been given. It is easy to forget what you do have and only focus on what is missing from your life. Traveling can help put things back into perspective and re-center your priorities on what truly matters.

Consider traveling through an area that has no electricity or running water if you come from a place where cold bottled water is easily accessible and nearly anything you want can be delivered to your door in less than an hour. These are two completely different worlds and ways of living. For people who experience a more privileged quality of life, seeing others who live in drastically different situations can help you appreciate what you have and spark an interest for you to lend support to people living elsewhere.

> Find Truth: There's concept, and then there's experience. You can know things from reading them online and listening to a lecture, but to experience something in person is different.

Traveling can help open your eyes to the true kindness and goodness of humanity. There is a myth that when you travel you are on your own, but that simply is not the case. The welcoming attitude and overwhelming hospitality that people give to travelers may be one of the most surprising truths about traveling. Beyond that, you have the whole world to learn about with every place you discover, through every person you meet and every culture you experience.

> Expand Your Mind: A key benefit of traveling, or taking the opportunity to explore on a vacation, is being given the opportunity to expand your mind in ways you can't imagine. If you can allow yourself to travel with an open mind and accept the new experiences and adventures around you, you give your mind the chance to see the world from a new perspective.

Think of it as a spiritual and intellectual enlightenment. You never stop being curious and should always seek out education whenever possible throughout your life. You are doing a disservice to yourself if you choose to close yourself off from the world. It is not always easy to let new ideas in, especially when they are in direct contrast with what you may believe. You have everything you need to grow, you just have to allow yourself to do it.

> Connect to Others: It's easy to forget how similar you are to others, regardless of where you come from, what your background is, or how much money you have. At the end of the day, human beings share more in common with one another than they may choose to admit. When taking a trip to a different country, you may have learned to cast aside what is different and unusual because from the outside, others may not look or act alike. But if you give yourself a chance, you may be surprised to find how minimal and superficial these differences are.

As you notice how you share similar needs, your perspective of your home expands, you become friends with people from different backgrounds and cultures, you realize how everyone is connected. This state of awareness is a jump in consciousness that can help you experience a world-centric view of consciousness more expansive and aware.

> Break Out of Your Shell: Without a doubt, one of the benefits of traveling is that it forces you to step out of your bubble, which can provide you with many emotional health benefits. Yes, it may be uncomfortable and scary to break away from your daily routine, but the rewards are worth it. What you gain in experience and knowledge may outweigh any amount of doubt or apprehension you had before embarking on your journey. Travel also helps you to self-reflect and dig deep into who you are as a person.

Something magical happens when people are put in new situations than they are normally faced with in their everyday life, as behavior becomes more raw and real as a result of being out of your conditioned environment. This not-so-subtle push into the world helps you to become more open and comfortable expressing yourself without the worry of feeling judged.

> See the Big Picture: Life is a limited gift. You must choose to make the most of each day. As you travel and experience more of the world, you may be struck with gratitude and appreciation for all the places you have enjoyed and people you've shared your travels with. You have the power to take control of your life and can inspire you to start doing more.

Jesse Russell

Liechtenstein Introduction

A pocket-sized principality in the heart of Europe, Liechtenstein rarely tops anybody's bucket list of continental must-sees. Yet this tiny, landlocked nation offers more than you'd imagine: from long-standing history to sky-high mountains; cliff-hanging castles to odd cultural quirks.

Many of Liechtenstein's historical highlights are located in the capital, Vaduz. While this tiny town may only have around 5,000 inhabitants, it also boasts an array of fascinating museums and galleries including the Liechtenstein National Museum, the Museum of Fine Arts and the FIS Ski and Winter Sports Museum as well as the atmospheric Prince's Wine Cellars and the neo-Gothic Vaduz Cathedral. All these attractions are watched over by the pretty Vaduz Castle, which remains the official residence of the Prince of Liechtenstein.

Vaduz isn't Liechtenstein's only town of historical note. The second town, Schaan, is actually larger than Vaduz, and comes with its very own impressive church and Roman remains, while Balzers in the south west boasts what is perhaps Liechtenstein's most arresting fortification. There are also beautiful chapels to be found in lesser-visited villages like Triesen and Planken.

And yet the true star of Liechtenstein is the remarkable nature. This country has arguably the most impressive landscape in Europe. Most of the peaks in Liechtenstein soar more than 2,000m (6,562ft) into the sky, making Liechtenstein a premier destination for skiing, hiking and mountain biking. Its shimmering lakes are also a big draw for swimmers.

As well as its permanent attractions, Liechtenstein also excels when it comes to unusual events. Some of the fun annual highlights include the Monster Concert (where troupes of musicians and dancers dress in outlandish costumes and bang drums), the Cattle Drive (where cows and sheep are festooned in colourful garments and adorned with bells) and the LGT Alpine Marathon (where competitors from around the globe run for 26 miles through the mountains).

Factor in Liechtenstein's dynamic dining, drinking and live music offerings, and you have a pocket sized nation that punches well above its weight.

About Liechtenstein

Guide to Liechtenstein

Liechtenstein sightseeing. Travel guide attractions, sights, nature and touristic places

The size of this unique European country is smaller than many capitals. Despite that, Lichtenstein never ceases to amaze its guests with its unforgettable beauty and numerous nature and historical sights. One fifth of the country's territory is covered by forests. Vineyards, spacious pastures, agriculture fields and small charming villages and towns can be seen everywhere in the country.

The majority of towns are concentrated in the Rheine River region. Here tourists will see numerous old buildings with unusual tiled roofs, beautiful bridges and boulevards. An interesting peculiarity there is a flower bed in front of nearly every house. There are so many flowers in towns of Lichtenstein that towns look more like big blooming gardens.

The most interesting historic buildings can be found in the city of Vaduz, the capital of Lichtenstein. During the medieval period, the city was used as an important protective point. At that time, the city looked more like a big fortress. The remaining buildings of that period can be found in the old part of the city. Vaduz Castle, the official residence of the Prince of Liechtenstein, is the most notable landmark of the city. The castle was built in the 9th century. The first hotel in the country is also located in Vaduz and it is still working. It is named Gasthof Lowen hotel, and it is highly valued by its guests due to luxurious historic design. There is a large vineyard right in front of the hotel. Best sorts of grape are grown here to be turned into amazing wine at the local vinery.

When it comes to describing wine, we simply cannot fail to mention the importance of Vaduz Vinery that is known as one of the best vineries in Europe. This is not only a place to sample amazing wine, but also a beautiful architectural landmark. The buildings of the vinery were constructed several centuries ago and are surrounded by magnificent parks and groves. The National Museum remains the biggest cultural facility in the country. In the museum, visitors will find collections of coins, weapons, folklore items and other precious artefacts.

A visit to the Museum of Post Stamps will be no less interesting. Some of the items exhibited date back to the beginning of the 20th century. Art connoisseurs are recommended to visit the Art

Museum that exhibits many precious drawings by famous artists. Finally, a town of Triesenberg is a great place to attend several interesting excursions. Experienced guides will show you several historic churches, magnificent nature parks and the local Museum of Ethnography.

History and Entertainment

Just like other modern European countries, Liechtenstein was a part of the Roman Empire over 2 000 years ago. In the first half of the 6th century, the country was conquered by the Franks. Liechtenstein had been a part of the Kingdom of the East Franks until 911. When the kingdom collapsed, it became a part of the Duchy of Swabia. Exactly this period was marked by the country's struggle for independence. At the beginning of the 19th century, Liechtenstein was a part of the German Confederation and gained independence from it in 1866.

Enchanting landscapes, tiny towns, a diversity of historical attractions and cultural venues – this all attracts thousands of travelers to visit this pocket country. On the territory of the country, there is a famous resort of Malbun. It is more suitable for beginners but experienced skiers will not be bored here too. The resort includes 4 black routes. There are over 20 ski routes for beginners. There are also 2 ski schools. This is a perfect place for family recreation.

Liechtenstein may be also interesting for fans of food tourism. The main peculiarity of the local cuisine is a diversity of farmer products. A lot of food traditions have been borrowed from neighboring countries. At classical national restaurants, you can taste fondue and fois gras that traditional dishes in neighboring Switzerland. The main gems of the national cuisine are farmer cheeses and meat delicacies being produced here for many hundreds of years.

In the vicinity of this pocket country, there are also several outstanding attractions, to which you can take a trip. One of such places is the Three Sisters – three fascinating rocky peaks. This beautiful mountain is located on the border between Liechtenstein and Austria. The highest of its peaks is 2053 m. At one of the peaks, you can see ruins of the ancient castle built in the 9th century.

Fans of historical excursions can take an interesting trip to the Gutenberg Castle. It is located close to the border with Switzerland. The castle was built on the cliff top and has several interesting features. The architecture of the castle implies that it seems incredibly tiny from the distance and surprises with its impressive size and monumentality at close range.

Soul of Liechtenstein
Languages & religions
Religions and languages in Liechtenstein

The official language of Liechtenstein is German. Statistics show that the principality is the smallest state in Europe, in which the German language prevails. To date, there are no official set out regional languages in Liechtenstein, and no rights in terms of languages have been granted to national minorities. Despite the fact that Liechtenstein converse in German, literary Swiss is the written language. The basic rules of spelling in it are somewhat different from the standard classical German language. Such a confusion of the two linguistic groups was most likely a consequence of Liechtenstein's territorial location and Switzerland's influence on its formation as a state.

The media is required to use German in their activities. Also, only this language is employed in the education process in schools, as well as in literature production and issuing public documents and covenants. Representatives of the authorities are also supposed to communicate using the language. The most common local dialect of the German language is the Alemannic dialect. According to statistics, about 90% of all residents of the dwarf state are native speaker of the Alemannic dialect. Also in some regions of the country, one can find a similar dialect called Gorno-Aleman (Gornoalemansky) or Upper Aleman dialect (Verkhnealemannsky). Generally, all these small language units are employed only in Liechtenstein. Hence, world linguists for the sake of convenience classify all these dialects as one single Liechtenstein dialect.

The history of the formation of the national language begins from the 13th century of our era. Before that time, the population of modern Liechtenstein was divided into two equal language groups. One of them was native speakers of the Alemannic dialect, and the second – the Romansh language. Due to the influence of the Kingdom of the Franks, this bilingualism almost completely disappeared and the local population eventually began to converse exclusively in the Alemannic dialect. It is worth noting that at present, there are still residential areas in Liechtenstein whose names were derived from the Celtic language. The reason for this is that before the Romans conquered the territory, the Celts ruled this area and many historical names stuck.

In addition to the German language, the Italian language is widely spoken in the country. More than 1% of the local population considers it their native language. There are also citizens who speak Portuguese, Turkish, Spanish and Albanian. However, the number of these communities does not exceed 250 people each. Talking about the religious situation in the society, Liechtenstein is also a homogeneous country. Almost all the believing local population consider themselves Christians, but there are different directions of this religious teaching here. The main denomination is Catholicism. It is practiced by about 77% of the population according to data for the previous year.

It is worth noting that as of 6 years ago, Liechtenstein supported the religious activities of the relevant organizations and allocated grants to support this sphere of life. However, since 2011 the government has started to develop a special bill that deprived the church of state support and turned it into an independent structure. The entire Roman Catholic Church, which is operational in the territory of Liechtenstein, is part of the Catholic Universe and is subject to the Pope of Rome. In total, there are 11 parishes in the territory of the dwarf state, in which 19 diocesan priests serve.

All Catholic holidays are celebrated by local believers and they try to adhere to religious traditions. However, modern day youth is increasingly moving away from faith and the number of atheists in the state is gradually increasing. According to statistical data, a rather large percentage of Muslims live in Liechtenstein. They amount to about 1,500 people, which is more than 4% of the total population. Christians put up with Muslims and there have never been any confrontations between the two religious denominations. The next largest religious denomination is Buddhism, but it is practiced by less than 100 people. There is only one Buddhist center on the territory of the country.

Useful info

Best transportation means

***Travelling through Liechtenstein - roads, airports,
railway, bus transportation***

The transport interchange on the territory of
Liechtenstein is developed at a sufficiently high
level. The most popular type of public transport is
the bus. The density of routes of this mode of
transport is at maximum, notwithstanding the
specific terrain. The fare is much cheaper than in
most European countries. It should be noted that
even in those cities that do not have fully
functional bus stations, there are regular trips
according to a clear schedule. You can get
acquainted with it on the carrier's site or at the
bus stations in towns and villages. There is a well
developed cab service in the princedom. Despite
the fact that Liechtenstein is considered a dwarf
state, four different major railway stations are

located on its territory. The total length of the entire railway network is about 10 kilometers.

The railway is of international importance, since it links Liechtenstein with Switzerland and Austria. All trains run in strict accordance with the timetable. The cost of tickets depends on the time of the trip, the type of wagon and additional services. Due to the small size of the principality and the specific topography, air traffic is not developed at all. It is impossible to get to the country by air transportation; there is not even a single airport or runway here. The nearest airport is situated in Zurich, from which you can get to the Swiss border towns and from there by bus to Liechtenstein. Also, to get to the Principality, tourists often use the airport of St. Gallen-Altenrhein, which is located in Switzerland.

You have the opportunity to rent a car if you so desire. It is worth pointing out that right-hand driving is what operates on the territory of Liechtenstein. Furthermore, there are no toll roads. In residential areas, it is allowed to develop a speed of up to 50 km/h, and beyond them, up to 80 km/h. In order to rent a car, you need to have an international driver's license with you, as well as a credit card that will be used as collateral. Much attention is paid to safety in the country, hence the driver and all passengers must have their seatbelts fastened, and children under the age of 12 must be fixed with the help of special safety systems. During the trip, it is necessary to constantly keep your headlights on the dipped beam, since the roads in the Principality very often turn into tunnels.

Main airports and avia transportation
Railway, bus, water and other transport

Liechtenstein has a well-developed domestic transportation system. The most popular type of public transport is buses. All of them use the main highway, which runs along the Rhine River, and connects Austria and Switzerland. As a rule, there is a new run every 20 to 30 minutes, and in the largest tourist centers buses run at intervals of 7-10 minutes.Tickets can be purchased in advance via the internet, in special vending machines, in kiosks, as well as directly from the driver. If you intend to employ the services of public transportation quite often, it will be much more profitable for you to purchase what is called an unlimited monthly card. This card will operate for 7 days and costs about 12 Swiss francs. There is the opportunity to purchase such a travel card for a month or for a longer period. A one-time ticket will cost at least 3 francs, so buying a travel card can save you quite a lot.

Despite the fact that Liechtenstein has a pretty tight bus interchange, travelling by bicycle is the most popular mode of transportation among the local population. You can also take advantage of this mode of transportation, as they have rental offices located in all tourist places. It is possible to rent a car. For this, you will need to have an international driver's license and a credit card. The renter must be over 20 years of age. If you want to enjoy the picturesque landscapes of Liechtenstein, it is best to travel by train. There are four large railway stations in the country that pass through the entire country and connect it with Switzerland and Austria.

You can buy tickets in advance via the internet or at the ticket stands in railway stations. The technical condition of the wagons is at a high level .The fare depends on the class of the wagon, the time of day, and the day of the week of travel. The railway is classified under the Austrian department. There are taxis in the country, although they did not develop much due to the small territory of Liechtenstein. You can catch a cab on the road or order one by phone. You have to pay at least 5 francs for boarding and every kilometer ride will cost from 2 francs. As a rule, in the evenings, on holidays, as well as on weekends, the tariffs increase significantly

When to visit climate

Climate and best seasons to visit Liechtenstein. Actual weather forecast
Liechtenstein has a temperate continental climate. Some regions are characterized by the alpine climate zone which softens under the influence of wet and warm sea breezes. Winter in the country is quite cold although there are no strong frosts. Almost the entire winter period is accompanied by strong winds which are associated with a

multidirectional movement of air masses from the sea. The annual precipitation is about 1,300 millimeters. The summer months in Liechtenstein also features a moderate temperature. There is no exhausting heat here, yet the weather is not spoilt by the regular precipitation. Basically, every summer day is sunny and cloudless.

In the middle and late summer, strong winds which are accompanied by sharp pressure drops are observed in the territory of Liechtenstein. Note that due to the multidirectional movement of air masses on different slopes of the same mountain, the weather can be quite different. With the onset of winter, air temperature in Liechtenstein begins to fall gradually; on average it reaches 5°C throughout the territory. The sky is covered with clouds, precipitation falls regularly (rarely snow) and strong gusts of wind are possible. January in Liechtenstein is considered to be the coldest month of the year. In some regions, the air temperature can drop down to as low as -4°C. Also, January is characterized by fog, heavy rains, and snow which do not stay for a long time on the surface.

With the arrival of February, the air temperature starts to rise again and on average reaches 8°C. From the month of March, cloudy days will gradually begin to give way for sunrise. The air temperature during this time reaches 13°C and in April it is already 17°C. Despite the fact that until the end of spring the temperature only rises, it is usually in May that the greatest amount of precipitation is recorded. One should keep this in mind when planning a trip. In June, the air temperature reaches 23-24°C on average and the number of sunny days becomes significantly more than in May. At this time the water temperature is 19°C. The hottest month in Liechtenstein is considered to be July, when the temperature can rise up to 27°C. Autumn in the country is characterized by an average temperature of 9°C and a cloudy weather.

Top periods for vacation in Liechtenstein

Liechtenstein, despite its rather modest territorial size, is a popular tourist destination, as you can perfectly relax here at any time of the year. The peak of the tourist season comes naturally from the end of autumn and lasts until the beginning of spring, for the reason that this country is considered the center of skiing and extreme winter sports. Mild winter and the specific terrain of the country made it possible for ski resorts to create the most comfortable high-quality infrastructure for the winter holidays. Also in winter, hiking tours in the Alps and adjacent valleys are popular. Quite often, tourists come to Liechtenstein to celebrate the New Year and Christmas holidays. At this time, grandiose events and colorful festivals are held here, which will allow you to get acquainted with the traditions of the local population.

It is worth noting that Liechtenstein is one of the safest countries in the world, which is why people happily come here with children on New Year or summer holidays. If the purpose of the trip is shopping, then it is worth visiting during the off-season, in September-October, and also from March to the end of May. The fact is that the prices of goods here are among the highest in the whole of Europe. At the same time, prices grow with the increase in the number of tourists. Gastronomic tours are very popular in Liechtenstein. In order to try the local cuisine, you can visit the country at any time of the year. However, by the end of January in the big cities, there are incredible culinary festivals.

Despite the fact that Liechtenstein is quite a small country, a large number of cultural, historical and natural sights have been set up on its territory. That is why excursion tours are also popular in this direction. It is best to visit them in summer, as the weather during this period is quite warm, there is no exhausting heat and the amount of precipitation is minimal. Consequently, nothing prevents you from strolling through the old chapels, studying art galleries and visiting museums. From the end of spring, tourists arrive in the country in order to go hang gliding. If you want to visit a grandiose musical festival in Liechtenstein, you should go there in July so as to make it to the legendary Guitar Day. On August 15th, the Day of Fireworks is held in the country. This event attracts young people from all neighboring countries.

Political life

Politics, constitution and administrative structure of Liechtenstein

Liechtenstein is a principality located in Central Europe. The country is a dwarfish state, since its area does not exceed 157 square kilometers. There is a hereditary monarchy based on constitutional and democratic principles in the country. The Constitution of the country was established in 1921 and since then amendments and additions have been made to it a couple of times. It is worth noting that the principality is dominated by a dualistic system of government. Therefore, both the head of Liechtenstein and the local population together represent the sovereignty of the country. The head of the country is the Prince, and he has quite broad powers. It is he who takes decisions on all the most important domestic and foreign policy issues. He too represents the principality in the international arena. It is also in the Prince's power to convene and even dissolve the parliament and sanction laws.

Any bill that was drafted by other structural bodies must be confirmed by the signature of the Prince. Also within his rights is mitigation of punishment, issuing a pardon or even suspension of an investigation. The main legislative body is the Landtag. It is formed by a little over twenty members who are elected by a secret ballot based on a proportional system. The term of office of each deputy is not more than 4 years. Absolutely all citizens of the country who have already reached the age of 20 are eligible to participate in the elections. It is worth noting that as of 35 years ago, women in Liechtenstein did not have the right to vote. However, after a change in the Constitution and some reforms, the rights of women and men have become equal, and they also have the right to participate in the election of political authorities.

After the parliament is formed, the prince consults with it and creates a coalition government. It consists of only 4 advisors, as well as their head. Three members of the Council come from the party that won the majority of votes in the last election, while the other two members represent the interests of the opposition bloc. It is worth noting that the Constitution stipulates a multi-party system. It is for this reason that several political organizations are operational within the territory of modern Liechtenstein. The predominant political structure is the Progressive Party. It has had a great influence on the political sphere of the country for many years and commands great respect among the local population. The Independent Party is also functioning successfully; they are of the center-right political direction.

Liechtenstein is divided into two districts. Local authorities are directly administered by the Government of the State. It is worth noting that the principality has been actively involved in various international organizations for many years and is the author of more than one international treaty. To date, Liechtenstein is considered one of the most successful members of the European Union. It is also a member of NATO, the UN, and representatives of the principality are members of the OSCE Mission. Based on its territorial location, Liechtenstein seeks to establish friendly relations with neighboring states. So about 100 years ago, a Customs Treaty was concluded, thanks to which the principality integrated in the common economic area with Switzerland.

This decision turned out to yield quite high dividends for Switzerland as well as for

Liechtenstein. In addition, after joining the European Union, the benefits of European economic area became available to Liechtenstein. The Constitution of Liechtenstein makes provision for an independent judiciary. It is worth noting that the judicial system in the country has only three levels. The lowest judicial authority is the district court. It is followed by the Supreme Court of Liechtenstein, which performs the role of the Appeal Court. The highest judicial body is the Supreme Court of the Principality. All judges are appointed personally by the head of state. However, the lists of candidates are made by the Minister.

All administrative issues are decided upon by a specially created Administrative Court. It considers questions about unlawful decisions of the government. In order to constantly monitor the observance of constitutional norms and

regulations, a body such as the Supreme State Tribunal was created. It protects the rights and freedom of citizens, which are written in the Constitution. It also has the power to resolve disputes between courts and administrative authorities, and is a disciplinary authority for all members of the government. According to labor legislation, various trade unions are allowed on the territory of the country. Today there are about two dozen them.

Economics and GDP

National economy of Liechtenstein industries, GDP and prosperity level

Despite the fact that Liechtenstein is a dwarfish state and has access to limited reserves of natural resources, it is considered as an economically developed industrial country that excels in marketing and guarantees its citizens a decent standard of living. In general, Liechtenstein's economy is diversified and is divided into a large number of different small enterprises. In order to create the most comfortable conditions for the development f business within the country, the government reduced tax rates, which now amount to a maximum of 20%. They also simplified the registration scheme for new business units.

It is worth noting that there is a shortage of labor in Liechtenstein today. This led to the development of manufacturing industries and the steady growth of small businesses in the territory of the principality. In total, more than 32,000 people are today employed in various spheres of activity, and this is despite the fact that at least 12,000 of them are not citizens of Liechtenstein and come to work daily from Austria and Switzerland.

The most able-bodied population is employed in the service sector, about 40% are employed in the industrial sector and less than 2% are employed in the agricultural sector. A significant contribution to the development of the economy is made by the tourism sector. Thanks to the peculiarities of the climatic zone and relief, the country has created the most comfortable conditions for the development of ski resorts, which now enjoy incredible popularity. Many of them have no equal in the world.

The agricultural sector is focused on the production of meat and dairy products, which mostly satisfy the needs of the local population. In some cases, the surplus is exported. In addition, the country grows various grains, as well as potatoes and some vegetables. In view of the favorable climate, Liechtenstein was able to develop winemaking. On the slopes of the mountains grows lots of grapes of different varieties, and next to the valleys are wineries. Most of their products go to the domestic market and less than half to export. It should be noted that the manufacturing industry has developed well on the territory of the country. Precise mechanical engineering has been actively

developing for the last eight years. Swiss companies invest in this sector, and they also open their branches in Liechtenstein.

It is worth noting that the country dwarf is one of the advanced manufacturers of dental prostheses made of ceramics. Besides this, the country produces high-quality surgical instruments, as well as tools that are used for making jewelry, electronics and microelectronics. The automobile manufacturing industry in Liechtenstein is not developed, so most cars are purchased from neighboring Germany, Austria or Switzerland.

To date, the country's economy largely depends on foreign markets. The exported products include ceramics, postage stamps, which make a significant contribution to GDP, as well as precision instruments and electronics. The main countries with which Liechtenstein conducts trade relations are members of the European Union, as well as Switzerland, with which an agreement on a common economic and trade area was concluded about 100 years ago.

In the field of imports, in addition to cars, food products, textiles, as well as metal structures and machinery are predominant. The main import partners are also the countries of the European Union and Switzerland. It is worth noting that, regardless of its size, the principality managed to achieve development in the export sector. So today, the cost of export is at least three times higher than the cost of imports and the income from it is about $2.7 million. Due to the low percentage of taxation and comfortable conditions for business registration, many foreign companies register their organizations in Liechtenstein. Such a policy also contributes to a significant economic growth and makes an invaluable contribution to GDP.

The transport system of the country is focused exclusively on transit transportation. The main railway line of Liechtenstein connects Zurich and Innsbruck. Due to the fact that Liechtenstein is located between large and economically successful countries, transit by roads and railways generates a very high income. Despite the fact that Liechtenstein's monetary policy is aimed at stabilizing the financial situation of the country, there has been a significant budget deficit in recent years; spending exceeds revenues by at least $200,000. To date, GDP per capita is $27,000.

The inflation rate is about 0.5% and unemployment rate is 1.8%.

The History

Early history

The region that is today Liechtenstein was first inhabited in the fifth millennium before the Common Era. In the first half of the first millennium of the Common Era it formed part of the Roman Empire, with the Dominion of Schellenberg and the County of Vaduz later becoming regions of the German Empire with imperial immediacy.

Archaeological finds have shown that the region that is today Liechtenstein has been inhabited since the Neolithic Age (5th millennium before the Common Era). As the freeflowing Rhine would have made it hard to live on the valley floor, first settlements were created on raised areas of land.

For example, there is evidence of a settlement on the hilltop that is home to Gutenberg Castle in Balzers as well as in Eschnerberg. In the year 15 BC the Romans defeated the Rhaetians and created the Roman province of Raetia. In the first century BC an army road connecting Milan and Bregenz was built over the Luzisteig and along the right bank of the Rhine. This road led to the construction of estates and forts in the region occupied by modern-day Liechtenstein.

The creation of the County of Vaduz

The fall of the Roman Empire resulted in the Alemannic people moving into the area. In the 8th century Raetia became part of the Frankish Kingdom and in the 10th century part of the Alemannic Duchy. At this time the region was ruled by the Counts of Bregenz. On 3 May 1342 it was divided, creating the County of Vaduz. In the decades and centuries that followed, the County was to be the backdrop to much fighting and pillaging, including during the Swabian War (1499-1500).

Refoundation of Liechtenstein

After being ruled by various different noble families (Counts of Werdenberg, Sulz, Brandis, Hohenems), Schellenberg and Vaduz were purchased by Prince Johann Adam in 1699 and 1712 respectively. In 1719 they were merged and raised to the status of an Imperial Principality, before becoming a sovereign state in 1806. The 19th century was marked by great poverty that resulted in many people leaving the country, mostly for the USA.

The last counts to rule the area today known as Liechtenstein were the Counts of Hohenems. It was under their rule that the witch trials were held. Due to their large debts they were forced to sell the County of Vaduz and the Dominion of Schellenberg. In 1699 Prince Johann Adam purchased the Dominion of Schellenberg and in 1712 the County of Vaduz. The two territories were united via an imperial diploma issued by Emperor Karl VI on 23 January 1719, creating an Imperial Principality bearing the name Liechtenstein. As this new country only comprised small farming villages, the administrative authority was established in the nearest town, Feldkirch, where the Prince built the Palais Liechtenstein for the administrative staff.

Liechtenstein's independence

Over the course of history Liechtenstein has been occupied by foreign troops on several occasions. During the War of the First Coalition (1792-1797) French soldiers entered the country; after battles between Austria (with support from Russia) and France, Liechtenstein was occupied by Napoleonic troops during the War of the Second Coalition (1799-1802). In 1806 Napoleon accepted the country as one of the founding members of the Confederation of the Rhine, thereby making Liechtenstein an independent state. This independence was confirmed at the Vienna Congress, with Liechtenstein becoming a member of the German Confederation.

Liechtenstein developed slowly and remained underdeveloped for many years. The revolution in 1848 did not lead to an immediate change in the situation. It was not until the customs treaty with Austria in 1852 that economic conditions began to improve, with the 1862 constitution bringing about political change by placing for the first time restrictions on the Prince's power to rule.

20th century

The early 20th century marked a major political turn in Liechtenstein. The lawyer Wilhelm Beck, who had studied in Switzerland, demanded that the Prince give more power to the people. He received much support, particularly among workers, and this resulted in a new constitution being drawn up in 1921. The Customs Treaty signed with Switzerland in 1923 and the introduction of the Swiss franc as the official currency in Liechtenstein had a positive economic effect on the country.

Though Liechtenstein remained neutral during the First World War, the country felt the economic impact of the conflict. The population became increasingly poor. Following the end of the war Liechtenstein split from Austria and intensified its relations with Switzerland, culminating in the 1923 Customs Treaty. Liechtenstein also suffered great poverty during the Second World War. Major public projects, such as the construction of the canal, were introduced in order to combat this poverty.

In 1938 Prince Franz Josef II became the first Prince to move his residence to Vaduz Castle, which has been the official residence of the Reigning Prince ever since.

Post-war economic boom

The first in a new wave of industrial companies were founded during the Second World War, while the post-war era was characterised by a prolonged economic boom that saw Liechtenstein transformed in the space of just a few decades from an agrarian state to a modern country with a diversified economy. The highly specialised industrial companies based in Liechtenstein today compete on a global level, with manufacturing playing an important role in the region.

The rebuilding of the economy after the Second World War was followed by accession to the statute of the International Court of Justice in 1950. In 1975 Liechtenstein became one of 35 states to sign the Helsinki Final Act of the CSCE (today OSCE). In 1978 Liechtenstein joined the Council of Europe and in 1990 it became a member of the United Nations (UN). It joined the European Free Trade Association (EFTA) as a full member in 1991 and has been a member of the European Economic Area (EEA) and the World Trade Organisation (WTO) since 1995. Relations within the framework of the EEA and the EU are of particular importance to Liechtenstein's foreign policy, economy and European integration.

Maintaining good bilateral relations with neighbouring Switzerland and Austria is also important.

The People

Liechtenstein is the fourth-smallest country in Europe and lies in the heart of the Alps between Switzerland and Austria. It is the sixth-smallest country in the world with a population of around 38,000.

Population

As of 31st December 2015, Liechtenstein had a total of 37,623 inhabitants. Around two thirds (66.3%) were born in Liechtenstein; a fifth of the population (19.4%) living in the country comes from other German-speaking countries (9.7% from Switzerland, 5.8% from Austria and 3.9% from Germany). The rest (14.3%) coming from other countries. The permanent population living in Liechtenstein includes citizens of around 90 different countries.

Demography

Liechtenstein's permanent population increased by 304 persons (0.2%) in 2017. On 31 December 2017 it had a population of 38,114.

The average age of the permanent population increased in 2014 by 92 days. As of 31 December 2014, the average citizen in Liechtenstein was 41.42 years old. The average age of women living in the Principality was 42.31 years, 1.80 years higher than the average age of men (40.51 years).

In 2011, life expectancy at birth was 84.2 years for women and 79.5 years for men. There were 133 more births than deaths, with the population growing by a total of 363 persons in 2012. The number of persons getting married increased slightly in 2012 from 324 to 348. In 2012, 119 persons resident in Liechtenstein and 55 persons resident outside Liechtenstein received citizenship of the Principaliy of Liechtenstein, an increase of 4 persons compared with the previous year. The 2010 census counted 10,337 buildings and 15,474 households. 3,500 Liechtenstein citizens live abroad in over 63 different countries.

Languages

German is the sole official language in Liechtenstein. In day-to-day affairs, Middle Alemannic and High Alemannic dialects are used. The Liechtenstein version of standard German can be compared with the standard German spoken in the Austrian province of Vorarlberg.

Those with a trained ear will be able to differentiate the many different dialects spoken in Liechtentein. Until a few years ago it was even possible to tell which municipality a person was from simply by listening to them speak. Today it is still possible to tell the difference between those from the Unterland and those from the Oberland.

Of the dialects spoken in the Oberland, those used in Balzers and Triesenberg are particularly easily recognisable as they are "Walser dialects". From a lexical point of view there are few differences since all dialects spoken in Liechtenstien originate from Upper German.

The differences are to be found in the pronunciation and, in some cases, in the speaking speed. The dialect spoken in Triesenberg is very Alemannic and contains some sounds that come from Old High German, while the dialects spoken down in the valley are closer to standard Alemannic and Upper German. The most obvious difference is in the pronunciation of the Middle High German sound "ei", which has been maintained in its original form in Triesenberg but is spoken in a range of different ways down in the valley. A good example is the Middle High German word "leitere", which means "ladder" ("Leiter" in standard German): in the various different dialects spoken in the valley you will hear "Läätara", "Lootara" or "Laatara".

For many years now there has been a trend among children growing up in Liechtenstein towards speaking Swiss German. This is in part due to the influence of Swiss German media and to primary school teachers speaking Swiss German. Teenagers in Liechtenstein also have their own way of speaking, which is similar to a moderated version of the youth slang heard in Zurich.

Religions

According to the constitution, the Roman Catholic church is the national church of Liechtenstein. As such, it enjoys the complete protection of the state. Following a recommendation by the Prince, efforts are currently underway to separate the church and state. However, the relationship between the two is often complex, particularly when it comes to ownership of land and property. A commission has been set up in order to reach a compromise.

As of 20 December 2012, every Liechtenstein citizen aged 14 years and over is free to choose his/her religious belief without the approval of a parent or guardian. In 2010, 79.9% of the population were Roman Catholic, 8.5% were Evangelical and 5.4% were Islamic. Until 1997, Liechtenstein belonged to the diocese of Chur. Following opposition from Christians in this diocese to the bishop Wolfgang Haas from Liechtenstein, the Pope created the archbishopric of Vaduz. Wolfgang Haas became archbishop in Vaduz, with the St Florin parish church in Vaduz being raised to the status of a cathedal church.

The Principality is home to two small Protestant churches that are organised as an association. One of these is Evangelical and the other Evangelical Lutheran. The Islamic community does not have an official mosque or an official cemetery in Liechtenstein, though efforts are underway to change this.

Healthcare system

Today, Liechtenstein's healthcare system meets the healthcare standards of a modern state. All citizens aged 16 years or older must have health insurance. The high number of general practitioners and specialist doctors and the relatively small population mean that citizens enjoy excellent healthcare. In-patients are treated either in Liechtenstein's own hospital or in one of the hospitals in the surrounding region. Healthcare agreements have been established between Liechtenstein and these hospitals over the border.

Liechtenstein's healthcare system is closely linked to the country's economic and social situation. The first healthcare law ("Sanitätsgesetz") was passed in 1874 and set out the duties of the national doctor ("Landesphysikus") and the national veterinarean ("Landestierarzt"). Both act as experts for the government, with the national doctor responsible, among other things, for monitoring pharmacies and training midwives.

The 1921 constitution stipulated that the state is responsible for caring for the sick and combatting alcoholism. The second major healthcare law was passed in 1945 following the introduction of provisions on healthcare in schools (1935) and dental care in schools (1942). Regular check-ups were introduced in 1977, in particular for pregnant women and young children. In 2004 the Doctors' Act ("Ärztegesetz") and the Office of Public Health were introduced. This Office is in charge of coordinating the healthcare system on behalf of the government.

Welfare system

The Office of Social Services is responsible for the welfare system in Liechtenstein. Its main tasks are providing advice to those seeking help, protecting child welfare, distributing benefits and advising the government.

The welfare system in Liechtenstein was traditionally private and run by the church, with the state providing only basic services. However, the introduction of social security in the mid-1950s relieved the church of many of its duties. The welfare system became a safety net for all citizens who, for whatever reason, were unable or only partially able to earn a living.

However, there were earlier efforts by the state to provide welfare support. In 1836 an office for orphans was created; in 1845 a commission for the poor and a national poverty fund were introduced. According to the Municipalities Act of 1864 and the Poverty Act of 1869, welfare was the responsibility of the relatives, followed by the community. The situation improved with the introduction of poorhouses in 1870. In the 1921 constitution responsibility for welfare was transferred from the municipalities to the state. In 1931 provisions were introduced on welfare for the unemployed, tuberculosis sufferers, infants, the sick and the elderly. In 1932 provisions, financed using a range of funds, were created concerning youth welfare and mental healthcare.

Through these provisions each aspect of welfare was covered in one way or another. However, the Social Assistance Act of 1965 introduced coordination and a fundamental modernisation of the welfare system. This law created a legal right to assistance, and responsibility for welfare issues was moved from a person's "place of origin" ("Bürgerort") to their place of residence. In 1966 parliament created the Welfare Office, today known as the Office of Social Services. This authority is responsible for coordinating state welfare services. It is supplemented by a range of initiatives, most of which are financed by the state. These include the remedial health centre, family assistance, the women's refuge and the women's information centre (INFRA). Welfare costs are divided 50/50 between the state and the municipalities.

Family policy

Activities, measures and institutions, both state-funded and private, exist in Liechtenstein to promote child welfare, with emphasis placed on equal opportunities regardless of the child's background. Family policy is focused on the best interests of the child within its core family and extended family. Self-help and parental responsibility are supported.

Family policy in the modern sense of the term was once not needed. It was taken for granted that families were members and bearers of society. Help was only provided if the person responsible for bringing up the children (mother) became ill. In 1894 general provisions were introduced to support the sick, and in 1913 these were supplemented by new provisions for the sick and women who had recently given birth. Following Liechtenstein's rapprochement with Switzerland, most Swiss legal provisions on family affairs and marriage were also adopted in Liechtenstein. However, these provisions were only set out in the General Civil Code; it was not until 1974 that a law in its own right (Marriage Act) was introduced.

Financial support for families

Families have received financial support from the family allowances fund ("Familienausgleichskasse") since 1958. Until around 1940 only civil servants were entitled to family welfare payments, though some companies also granted workers with families financial support on a voluntary basis. Since 1999 single parents have been entitled to additional financial support.

Family assistance
Inspired by a similar system in Switzerland, the municipalities in Liechtenstein introduced "family assistance associations" ("Familienhilfe-Vereine") in 1956. These provided assistance to households in cases of illness or accident. In 1966 these individual associations merged. Financing was provided through membership fees, donations from foundations and public funding. In 2013 a centralised coordination system was introduced, meaning that assistance for households

throughout Liechtenstein is coordinated by a single office.

Clubs and societies

Liechtenstein has a long tradition of clubs and societies. There are institutions for everything from sport and culture to volunteering. The first societies created in Liechtenstein were introduced in the middle of the 19th century and focused on culture (music, singing).

In the early 20th century the first theatre societies emerged in Liechtenstein. There were also reading clubs, mostly organised by the church. Today, however, the majority of clubs and societies are related to sport. As early as the 1930s young men in Liechtenstein played football. With very little infrastructure available in the country, they simply found an appropriate area of land and organised games, albeit rarely with a proper leather ball.

Winter sports also date back to the 1930s, and Liechtenstein even competed in the 1936 Winter Olympics. This was followed by the creation of luge and cycle clubs, with fans of more modern sports also creating clubs and societies in recent years.

There are almost too many clubs and societies in Liechenstein to count. Pretty much every hobby or area of interest has its own organisation, ranging from sport and culture to volunteering. Whereas clubs and societies used to exist within a community, these days most include people from several villages interested in the same hobby.

The carnival societies ("Fasnachtsvereine") are among the oldest societies in Liechtenstein. They organise carnival parades and write carnival newspapers. In many cases they were created from other clubs and societies.

Geography

Around half of Liechtenstein lies in the mountains (Central Alps), with the highest elevation the Grauspitz at 2599 metres above sea level. (The lowest elevation is Ruggeller Riet at 430m.) The Naafkopf mountain lies on the border between Liechtenstein, Austria and Switzerland. The peaks in the alpine areas are part of the Limestone Alps, while those belonging to the Fläscherberg and Eschnerberg chains are part of the Helvetic zone.

Location

Liechtenstein enjoys a position in the heart of Europe on the banks of the Rhine between Germany, Austria and Switzerland. It takes only an hour by car to reach the city of Zurich and its international airport. Business meetings in Munich and shopping trips in Milan are just a two-hour drive away.

Despite its small size, Liechtenstein is a very attractive location in the heart of Europe on the banks of the Rhine between Switzerland and Austria. Excellent transport connections with both of these countries make it easy to get to Liechtenstein.

Good transport links
The airports in Zurich (CH), Munich (GER) and Innsbruck (AT) are a maximum of two hours away. Buses run regularly from the railway stations in Feldkirch (AT), Buchs SG (CH) and Sargans SG (CH) to Liechtenstein, with timetables designed to match the arrival times of trains at these stations. The bus network within the country is also very good regular buses make it easy to travel to any of the municipalities. While Liechtenstein does not have its own motorway, the network of roads is comprehensive. Drivers in a hurry to get from Balzers in the south to Ruggell in the north can use

the "Rheintalautobahn" motorway on the Swiss side of the Rhine.

Climate

Liechtenstein lies between the Lake Constance climate zone (wet and cool, influenced by the Atlantic) and the dry, warm Inner Alpine climate zone around the Swiss town of Chur. The Principality receives relatively little precipitation and enjoys high average temperatures thanks to the influence of the Föhn wind.

While for many people the Föhn is a nuisance, causing aches, pains and fatigue, others love the warm wind and the special atmosphere it creates. Known in Liechtenstein as the "grape cooker", it is particularly popular with winemakers. The Föhn is a warm, dry katabatic wind that blows through Liechtenstein in certain climatic conditions. It results in an extended vegetation period in the country. The mountain chains that surround Liechtenstein create a climate typical of Inner Alpine areas protected by the mountains. The Föhn contributes not only to good grape harvests but also to excellent fruit-growing conditions.

The relatively low volume of precipitation (on average betwen 900 and 1200 ml), sometimes in combination with the influence of the Föhn, means that there is little snow in Liechtenstein. There are an average of around 1600 hours of sunshine per year. Those are the statistics. But in reality there are winters when residents need to clear snow every day, while in other years there is no need for the snow shovel at all. In summer, too, there are periods of warm and sunny weather lasting several weeks, but also cooler days with plenty of mist and fog. Liechtenstein has everything, even the different weather extremes!

Flora

Liechtenstein's flora can be divided into three zones: the Rhein Valley floor; the lower mountain slopes above the Rhine and the Alps; and the fens and moors. For many plants requiring warm conditions, Liechtenstein and the warm climate it enjoys, thanks in part to the Föhn wind, is the most northerly place they can flourish. Of the 1600 types of plants found in the Principality, 800 are native to mountainous regions. The country is also home to 48 different kinds of orchid as well as a wide range of flora in the Ruggeller Riet.

The first mention of Liechtenstein by a botanist dates back to 1537, when the German doctor and botanist Bock discovered the European cyclamen in the Oberland. Between 1896 and 1900 the Austrian botanist Beck created a herbarium with 500 plants for Liechtenstein. Other renowned botanists associated with Liechtenstein are Murr and Seitter, both of whom documented the various plants living in Liechtenstein. The most recent work of this kind was completed by Edith Waldburger from Buchs, who compiled a herbarium with all of the 1600 plants known to exist in Liechtenstein today. Of these 1600 plants, 25% are on the "Red List" of extinct, rare or endangered plants.

Diverse biosphere

Liechtenstein's moorland areas bear witness to the history of vegetation in the Principality following the Ice Age. Pollen trapped in peat remains intact for many millennia. The most important discovery of ancient pollen was found near the Obere Burg ruins in Rietle, Schellenberg. The most common tree in Liechtenstein after the Ice Age was the birch, followed by the fir and the hazel. Around 2000 years before the start of the common era, wheat was grown in the region - a sign that the area was inhabited or used by humans. After the end of the Ice Age, Liechtenstein was covered in forests, with the treeline at around 2000m altitude. The beech tree became the most prominent tree in the region and remains so today. The proximity of Liechtenstein to the area around the Swiss town of Chur meant that some plants native to that region also found their way into the Principality. The same goes for the Seeztal valley in the Swiss canton of St. Gallen. The Ruggeller Riet, a nature reserve which has been the subject of many publications, is well worth a visit. The Alps are also home to many interesting plants, in particular the tiger lily.

Flora

Liechtenstein's flora can be divided into three zones: the Rhein Valley floor; the lower mountain slopes above the Rhine and the Alps; and the fens and moors. For many plants requiring warm conditions, Liechtenstein and the warm climate it enjoys, thanks in part to the Föhn wind, is the most northerly place they can flourish. Of the 1600 types of plants found in the Principality, 800 are native to mountainous regions. The country is also home to 48 different kinds of orchid as well as a wide range of flora in the Ruggeller Riet.

The first mention of Liechtenstein by a botanist dates back to 1537, when the German doctor and botanist Bock discovered the European cyclamen in the Oberland. Between 1896 and 1900 the Austrian botanist Beck created a herbarium with 500 plants for Liechtenstein. Other renowned botanists associated with Liechtenstein are Murr and Seitter, both of whom documented the various plants living in Liechtenstein. The most recent work of this kind was completed by Edith Waldburger from Buchs, who compiled a herbarium with all of the 1600 plants known to exist in Liechtenstein today. Of these 1600 plants, 25% are on the "Red List" of extinct, rare or endangered plants.

Diverse biosphere

Liechtenstein's moorland areas bear witness to the history of vegetation in the Principality following the Ice Age. Pollen trapped in peat remains intact for many millennia. The most important discovery of ancient pollen was found near the Obere Burg ruins in Rietle, Schellenberg. The most common tree in Liechtenstein after the Ice Age was the birch, followed by the fir and the hazel. Around 2000 years before the start of the common era, wheat was grown in the region - a sign that the area was inhabited or used by humans. After the end of the Ice Age, Liechtenstein was covered in forests, with the treeline at around 2000m altitude. The beech tree became the most prominent tree in the region and remains so today. The proximity of Liechtenstein to the area around the Swiss town of Chur meant that some plants native to that region also found their way into the Principality. The same goes for the Seeztal valley in the Swiss canton of St. Gallen. The Ruggeller Riet, a nature reserve which has been the subject of many publications, is well worth a visit. The Alps are also home to many interesting plants, in particular the tiger lily.

Fauna

Despite its small size, Liechtenstein is home to an exceptionally wide range of animals. Around 55 mammals are native to Liechtenstein (Switzerland has 83), including 17 species of bat (26), 140 species of bird (205), 7 species of reptile (16), 10 species of amphibian (20) and 24 species of fish (67).

The great difference in altitude between the lowest elevation (430m) and the highest elevation (2599m) means that Liechtenstein is home to a very diverse range of fauna. In the Alpine area you will find most animals commonly found in mountainous environments, including the big four deer, chamois, ibex and golden eagle as well as the snow hare and the rock ptarmigan native to the northern Alps.

The transition from the valley floor to the mountains is characterised by forests. It is here that deer, foxes and badgers live, though they can also be found near the valley floor and at relatively high altitudes. The black woodpecker, the rare white-backed woodpecker and the eagle owl are all also native to these forests. While few of the animals living high in the mountains and in the forests further below are endangered, the situation is much more precarious in

Liechtenstein's wetlands. In an attempt to preserve what is left of these fens and marshes, the government has created two protected areas: Schwabbrünnen (50 hectares) and Ruggeller Riet (96 hectares). Wetlands are home to a wide range of plants and, as a consequence, form the habitat of many animals.

For example, a total of 408 species of beetle have been found in Ruggeller Riet. The area also has 82 species of spider, including 5 species that have only been found in a few other locations in the heart of Central Europe. Ruggeller Riet is also home to many species of bird. Around 30 species of nesting bird are native to the region as well as the globally endangered corncrake, the quail, the whinchat, the corn bunting and the common grasshopper warbler.

Geology and mountains

Around half of Liechtenstein's surface area lies in the mountains (Central Alps), with the highest elevation the Grauspitz at 2599 metres above sea level. (The lowest elevation is Ruggeller Riet at 430m.) The Naafkopf mountain lies on the border between Liechtenstein, Austria and Switzerland. The peaks in the alpine areas are part of the Limestone Alps, while those belonging to the Fläscherberg and Eschnerberg chains are part of the Helvetic zone.

Tectogenesis, the history of tectonic movements, can be clearly observed in Liechtenstein. Rocks in the Principality are almost exclusively made up of sea sediments originally from the Ancient Mediterranean Sea that once stretched from Central Europe to Guinea.

The geological end of the Eastern Alps
The Rätikon chain (westerly end of the Rätikon) also forms the geological end of the Eastern Alps.

The mountains are in part formed by a tectonic plate originally from the African region that has broken away and forced its way above and below the European sheets of the helveticum and flysch nappes. This tectogenesis includes folding, thrusting, expansion processes, the formation of fractures and tears as well as metamorphoses.

Today, the mountains in Liechtenstein comprise three layers with sediments from different seas. At the bottom lie the west alpine Limestone Alps, covered by a thick layer of flysch rocks. The top layer is the "Lechtaldecke" layer comprising several fault blocks.

Lakes and rivers

The Rhine, which forms 27km of the country's western border with Switzerland, is the most important river in Liechtenstein. The Samina in the Alps measures 12km and is the second-longest river (stream) in the Principality, running from its source in the Valünatal Valley before joining the Ill and flowing into the Rhine in Austria. The only natural lake is the Gampriner Seele, which was formed in 1927 when the Rhine burst its banks.

Liechtenstein has many more rivers than lakes. The "Binnenkanal" canal and the Spiersbach and Samina rivers transport excess water away from the country. The "Binnenkanal" has the largest drainage area (117km^2). Since completion in 1943 it has been used to transport the water that used to flow along the other rivers (except the Ruggeller Mölibach) directly into the Rhine. The Samina has a drainage area of 50km^2 in the mountains, the Spiersbach has a drainage area of 11km^2 in the north of the country.

Habitat for many animals and plants
The Gampriner Seele is the only natural lake in Liechtenstein and has a surface area of 1.53

hectares. The ponds in Hälos in Triesen (3.56 hectares) and Schwabbrünna-Äscher near Nendeln (0.4 hectares) are protected areas and important habitats for a wide range of animals and plants. The Spörriweier and the Steger Stausee reservoir were built to generate hydroelectricity.

Due to the destructive power of water, the country's rivers (in particular the Rhine) and rockfall have always been a source of potential danger. The swamp-like climate that existed on the valley floor until the 19th century contributed to the emergence of diseases such as malaria.

Water and its uses

Rivers and lakes have always been and are still used for various different purposes. As well as providing water, they were employed as early as the Middle Ages to generate energy (mills) as well as to transport people (Rhine) and wood (Samina). Fishing also used to be of great importance as a source of food. The dangers posed by the rivers have been significantly reduced through the construction of protection measures and dams. Defences have also been built to protect the population from rockfalls and avalanches.

Culture

160km^2, 37,000 inhabitants, 2,600 music pupils, 40 bands, 26 choirs, 10 brass bands, 2 orchestras, 2 musical theatres, 2 operetta stages and 1 opera company the facts and figures about music in Liechtenstein speak for themselves and show clearly that the Principality has one of the most active culture scenes in the world. In Liechtenstein, culture is all about doing, creating and experiencing. Embark on an exciting journey and discover the diversity of culture in Liechtenstein.

Culture policy

In Liechtenstein, culture policy is centered on the identity of the Principality and its inhabitants. The many institutions and local clubs make an important contribution towards enabling Liechtenstein's residents to identify with the country and its municipalities.

Its many active clubs and societies, cultural institutions, theatres and museums shape Liechtenstein and its cultural scene. Financial support from the state for projects and infrastructure is seen as contributing to the country's common identity and an investment in an open and successful community. Culture must be alive; culture must be lived.

Bridges to the past, foundations for the future
Looking forward also means looking back. That's why culture in Liechtenstein is just as much about building bridges to the past as laying the foundations for the present and the future.

Collections of cultural artefacts are silent witnesses showcasing the way in which countries and societies are constantly developing. Some objects date back only a few years, but in our fast-moving times they seem to belong to another era.

Freedom of expression, freedom of spirit
Culture in and from Liechtenstein is an exciting expression of the country's free spirit and a reflection of the society itself: it addresses current issues and celebrates the past; it is controversial yet blends into society; it maintains traditions and sets new trends.

Traditions

The word "tradition" sounds a little old-fashioned, a little outdated. But here in Liechtenstein we are proud of our local customs and our dialect; every year we look forward to the National Day and the carnival celebrations. Tradition is more than just a word traditions are the ideas and values passed on from generation to generation that form part of our lives and make us who we are.

Customs

Most of Liechtenstein's customs are drawn from Alemannic culture, with many also closely linked to the Catholic church and its holy days and rites. Customs are spread throughout the year and often mark the start or end of seasons or are even considered seasons in their own right.

The carnival season, referred to as "Fasnacht", is celebrated in Liechtenstein from Dirty Thursday through until Carnival Tuesday and is known as the "fifth season of the year". It is followed by Bonfire Sunday, traditionally the Sunday after Ash Wednesday, when a large pile of wood is set alight to drive away the winter. Liechtenstein's national day, the Prince's Day, is celebrated every year on

15 August. A holy day and a bank holiday in the Principality, it was introduced in 1940 and is closely linked to the birthday of the Reigning Prince at the time, Prince Franz-Josef II, on 16 August.

Bringing down the cattle wine harvest
After spending the summer grazing up on the high pastures, cattle are brought back down into the valley in autumn. This tradition is celebrated every year with small processions of cows being led through the villages with colourful headdresses made of flowers and bells around their necks. Many people gather to watch these processions, which are linked to traditional cattle markets in Triesenberg, Vaduz and Eschen that today take place in the form of fun fairs. Another autumn custom is the wine harvest, known as "Wimmlete". In the vineyards the grapes are gathered with the help of friends and relatives, before everyone

settles down over a hearty meal and a glass of wine to reflect on that year's harvest. The highlight of the annual "Wimmlete" is the measuring of the density of grape must according to the Oechsle Scale, an indication of grape ripeness and sugar content. If that year's harvest of Blauburgunder grapes reaches 100 on the Oechsle Scale, the winemakers celebrate by opening a few more bottles. Indeed, if the party is swinging and the wine is flowing then sometimes a score of only 90 is enough to justify a few more glasses.

Special traditions

Liechtenstein may be a small country, but its citizens are very proud of their local traditions. These can range from the language they speak to customs and values linked to the history of the Principality.

Liechtenstein's citzens speak an Alemannic dialect of German. Yet, despite the country's size, there is no "pure" Liechtenstein dialect. Instead, different variations of the dialect are spoken in the different regions an expression of the country's cultural diversity. Even today it is possible to tell which area of the country somebody is from simply by listening to them talk: Balzners, Triesenbergers and Ruggellers all speak in a certain way. A good example of this is the range of words used in Liechtenstein for "slippers", which can be called "Finka", "Tasi", "Tappa" and even "Pootscha" depending on where you are from.

Clichés and stereotypes
Liechtenstein's citizens may be proud of their traditions, but they also never miss a chance to tease their fellow countrymen about the local clichés and stereotypes passed down through the generations. It is said, for example, that those from

Balzers do everything very, very slowly; the common stereotype about people from the Unterland (north) of the country is that they own large amounts of land.

The "Scheidgraben"

Another cultural aspect peculiar to Liechtenstein is the "Scheidgraben". This term was originally used to refer to a ditch marking the border between the Oberland (south) and the Unterland (north). The ditch still exists today, and although it is not particularly deep it remains a symbol of the divide between the two regions that make up the country. On each side of the "Scheidgraben" you will hear different dialects, and the results of elections and referendums are often influenced by which side you live on. Liechtenstein was originally formed when the Dominion of Schellenberg (purchased in 1699, today the "Unterland") and the County of Vaduz (puchased in 1712, today the

"Oberland") were merged. That is why even today you will hear residents in the Unterland declare: "No Unterland, no fatherland."

One Princely House three generations
On 13 November 2014 Liechtenstein celebrated the 25th anniversary of Prince Hans Adam II taking the throne. To mark the 25th anniversary of H.S.H. Prince Hans Adam II succeeding to the throne and the 10th anniversary of H.S.H. Hereditary Prince Alois being installed as his representative, an interview was carried out with the three generations of the Princely Family Reigning Prince Hans Adam, Hereditary Prince Alois and 19-year-old Prince Wenzel

Legends
There is a long tradition in Liechtenstein of recounting legends and passing them on down through the generations. Many of these legends tell of fears and superstitions represented in the

form of devils, witches and natural spirits, while others explain how iconic parts of Liechtenstein's natural landscape (such as the "Three Sisters" mountain peaks) came to be.

On the Feast of the Assumption (15 August), three sisters went up to Gafadura above the village of Planken to pick berries. As they walked along the path they heard the sound of the church bells announcing the holy feast. One of the sisters suggested that they should go to church, but the other two replied that the baskets had to be full of berries before they returned to the village.

Towards the end of the afternoon the baskets were full and the sisters headed back home. On their way they met a beautiful woman who asked them for some berries. The sisters were reluctant to give her any and replied that people who want berries should pick them themselves. All of a sudden a halo appeared around the head of the woman and she spoke to them: "You have dishonoured my holy day and refused my request. Your hearts are of stone. Therefore, as a punishment, you shall be turned into stone and stay here forever." Upon saying that, the three sisters were transformed into huge rocks, which from that day on became known as The Three Sisters.

A legend for each municipality

Although there are some municipalities that are particularly well-known for their legends for example Triesenberg, Triesen and Balzers each of the eleven municipalities has its own legends. Often a legend is associated with a particular municipality because local buildings, people or areas of land are mentioned. "Die Jungfrau von Gutenberg" is from Balzers; "Die Tobelhocker" is from Triesen; "Die Wildmannli" is from Triesenberg; "Der Lochgass-Schimmel" is from

Vaduz; "Der Gritscher Poli" is from Schaan; "Der Geist bei der Kapelle" is from Planken; "Die goldene Boos" is from Eschen-Nendeln; "Der Pfandbrunnen" is from Mauren-Schaanwald; "Die Gampriner Rheinmühle" is from Gamprin; "Das Geisterhaus" is from Schellenberg; "Eine Hexe als Hund" is from Ruggell.

Food and drink

From traditional food made using seasonal produce to the finest haute cuisine, Liechtenstein's diverse culinary experiences including a selection of fine homegrown wines is a further characteristic of the country.

Many of the dishes traditional to Liechtenstein can be found in the "Liechtensteiner Kochbuch". Among the most popular are "Käsknöpfle mit Apfelmus", a doughy pasta dish with melted cheese served with apple sauce; "Ribel", a cornmeal-based dish served with a glass of milk, café au lait or sour cheese; and "Tatsch/Kratzete", a sweet, thick pancake served with compot. A homemade herb schnaps or fruit schnaps is recommended as a digestive to follow the hearty "Käsknöpfle".

Wine...
Years ago, many residents of Liechtenstein produced their own wine as an additional source of income, leading to the attitude "much wine is good wine". Today, however, winemaking in Liechtenstein is highly professional and the wines produced are of the very finest quality. The country is home to 100 winemakers, including four full-time professionals, who benefit from the climatic conditions in the Rhine Valley and the warm Föhn wind that ripens the grapes growing on the south-facing mountain slopes. The most

popular kinds of grapes in Liechtenstein include Pinot Noir and Müller-Thurgau.

and beer

After a wait of 90 years, Liechtenstein finally once again has its own beer. Since its creation in 2007 the microbrewery "Liechtensteiner Brauhaus" has brewed a selection of its own beers with great success. Several of the beers have won international prizes. In 2010 a second microbrewery, "Prinzenbräu", was also founded in Liechtenstein.

Theatre and dance

Theatre in all its forms is popular in Liechtenstein, not least amateur theatre. The country boasts a large number of passionate amateur actors and actresses who are often also frequent visitors to the professional productions put on in the Principality. Indeed, such is the attraction of the local theatre scene that many theatre enthusiasts from the surrounding region travel to Liechtenstein to attend performances. This also applies to the country's dance scene.

TAK Theater Liechtenstein
The "TAK" is the grand daddy of Liechtenstein's theatre scene. For over 40 years it has combined theatre, music, comedy, dance and readings under one roof. As well as staging its own productions, it frequently welcomes internationally renowned artists, ensembles, orchestras and conductors. Over the years it has developed into a platform for culture in Liechtenstein and today collaborates with the "Schlösslekeller" theatre and the "Literaturhaus Liechtenstein" to put on events.

Schlösslekeller good things come in small packages
The Vaduz cabaret stage, founded in 2003, is one of the "big" stages in Liechtenstein, not least

because of its move in November 2016 together with the TAK. The Schlösslekeller stands for an extremely lively cabaret scene in Liechtenstein, not only showing international and regional stars of the cabaret scene in its programme, but also promoting young local artists.

Junges Theater Liechtenstein
Every year since its foundation in 2001 the "Junges Theater Liechtenstein" has put on professional theatre productions featuring children, teenagers and adults with and without mental handicaps. Age groups range from U9 through to U21, with the theatre team on hand to introduce the children and teenagers to the world of acting in a fun and enjoyable way.

Amateur dramatics
Amateur dramatics are a major part of village life and have a long and proud tradition in Liechtenstein. Performances put on by the local

football team or the voluntary fire brigade draw large audiences and are annual highlights.

Music

While Balzers is known as "the village of song", Liechtenstein itself can most definitely be called the "country of music". If you could turn down the noises of everyday life, then somewhere in the country you could hear music being played by one of the many associations, bands, ensembles or orchestras.

Josef Gabriel Rheinberger

Liechtenstein composer and teacher Josef Gabriel Rheinberger (18391901) enjoyed great fame during his lifetime. His music was performed in some of the finest auditoriums in the world. While living in Munich he taught more than 600 music students from many different countries.

At the tender age of seven he played the church organ in his hometown of Vaduz. In 1851, aged twelve, he went to Munich to started studying music at the Royal Conservatorium. His talent quickly became clear as he wrote numerous works and soon outperformed his fellow students. At the age of 19 he was employed by the Conservatorium to teach piano and later organ and composition, a position he retained until shortly before his death. He was among the world's leading lecturers in composition. His pupils included Engelbert Humperdinck, Ermanno Wolf-Ferrari and Wilhelm Furtwängler.

Diverse oeuvre

Rheinberger's works include piano and organ music, church and secular choral music, solo songs, chamber music, symphonies, concert overtures and music for theatre and opera. He was one of the most successful composers of his time.

Many prizes and awards

In 1877 he acted as court conductor for King Ludwig II of Bavaria. This gave Rheinberger a central position within Catholic church music in Germany. His success is reflected in the many prizes and awards he received, including an honorary doctorate from the University of Munich.

The house where he was born, the "Rheinbergerhaus" in Vaduz, today houses the Liechtenstein Music School.

Liechtenstein Music School

A total of 2600 pupils attend Liechtenstein Music School. That is equivalent to 7% of the population, making Liechtenstein the country in Europe with the highest proportion of music pupils. Founded in 1963, the school offers a broad range of classes for all age groups. That means that almost everyone in Liechtenstein has some kind of connection to the Liechtenstein Music School during their lifetime.

Generous support from the national government and municipal councils when it comes to infrastructure and financing are proof of the importance of what is the largest education institution in Liechtenstein. In addition to the main music school, there are also two smaller music school centres in Triesen and Eschen that offer music enthusiasts of all ages excellent conditions for modern music teaching.

Diverse musical styles
Tuition at the Liechtenstein Music School covers both singing and instrumental music and encompases all genres, including classical and folk music as well as jazz, pop and rock. The members of staff are trained musicians with a diploma from a recognised higher education institution or academy of music.

The joy of making music together

Playing music together is a major part of life at Liechtenstein Music School and is promoted and supported accordingly. Performances and concerts put on by the school's choirs, ensembles, orchestras and bands contribute significantly to the cultural scene in Liechtenstein.

Liechtenstein International Masterclasses

The Liechtenstein International Masterclasses have been held since 1970. The list of international stars who come to Liechtenstein each summer to share their knowledge with around 100 up-and-coming musicians reads like a who's who of the music world. The traditional concerts put on by the teachers and pupils are one of the country's musical highlights each summer. Also of great importance is the International Music Academy, an institution created to support and promote talented young musicians.

From brass bands to the blues

As the working day draws to a close, the sound of music and singing fills the air in Liechtenstein. Nurses and carpenters join forces in the local brass band, lawyers and teachers perform Brahms's "In the Still Night" together, and with the members of his blues band an archaeologist grooves the night away.

Liechtenstein's long tradition of brass band music dates back to 1862, when the country's first brass band was founded in Triesen. Today there are ten bands and youth bands with around 1000 musicians represented in the Liechtensein Brass Music Society. Performances range from concerts and music at local events to the annual Liechtenstein Brass Music Society music festival.

36 choirs

Founded in 1919, the Princely Liechtenstein Singing Society ("Fürstlich Liechtensteinische

Sängerbund", FLSB) organises and coordinates the country's many choirs. It comprises 24 adult choirs and 12 children's choirs. All in all, more than 1000 singers practise every week. The highlight of Liechtenstein's choral scene is the bi-annual national song festival.

Classical music in Liechtenstein
The Liechtenstein Symphony Orchestra,

Liechtenstein-Werdenberg Orchestra and the orchestras of the Liechtenstein Music School are the flagships of classical music in Liechtenstein. They have made a name for themselves with concerts both within Liechtenstein and outside the country.

Jazz, blues, pop, rock
The Liechtenstein Blues and Rock Society heads the blues, pop and rock scene in Liechtenstein. On most weekends you will find at least one gig put on by the 60 or so bands in the Principality and the

surrounding region. The Liechtenstein Big Band has been at the heart of the country's jazz scene since it was founded in 1980 and is famous well beyond the national borders thanks to its concerts and recordings.

Art

Is art created for the artists themselves? For another person? For the general public? What is art? And why? A typical Liechtenstein answer to this question could be: "Stop asking, start doing!" That is exactly what art is: quiet, loud, intimate, public and most of all: diverse.

Art scene

Is art all about big ideas and big constructions? No, art lies in the eye of the beholder, even in little Liechtenstein. Art is not about size but about dexterity, creativity, heart and soul. That is what art is not only in Liechtenstein.

Art in Liechtenstein is not monumental, obvious art designed to be displayed in the world's major cities. Instead, it is a game of hide and seek. It creeps up on you and surprises you in public places, between shops, at the entrance to a building or as part of the architecture. There is plenty of art to discover just remember to keep your eyes open!

Advice, information and support
The Professional Association of Visual Artists ("Berufsverband Bildender KünstlerInnen") supports and protects Liechtenstein's burgeoning culture scene. It aims to promote all forms of visual art in Liechtenstein and represents the interests of its members in dealings with authorities and organisations at both at national and international level. It also provides information and advice for artists and art enthusiasts.

Vibrant art scene

Liechtenstein has a vibrant art scene. Artists from the Principality exhibit their work both at home and abroad and participate in many biennales, while film festivals, publications and exchange programmes with other countries are also a major part of the local art scene. Both the public and private sector frequently invest in ambitious architecture projects. Painters, graphic designers, video artists, sculptors, photographers and filmmakers all contribute to creating exciting and diverse art made in Liechtenstein.

Liechtenstein Cultural Foundation

Art is something to be nurtured and fostered not only during the good times. We need culture to live. It gives our lives sense. To make art is to create and shape something both in a material sense and a spiritual sense. A country's culture is the achievement of its people. It is this achievement that must be supported and promoted.

Culture in Liechtenstein is shaped by public institutions, private organisations and individuals. The latter includes artists from many different fields as well as the many citizens actively involved in cultural associations and societies.

Promote preserve support
Created on 1 January 2008, the Liechtenstein Cultural Foundation is committed to promoting cultural activities of individuals and private organisations in the fields of literature, music, performing and visual arts, audiovisual media, local culture and regional studies. A government institution, it aims to preserve the country's cultural diversity and to support artists and their work at as many levels as possible.

Museums and exhibitions

Museums are places where treasures are kept and showcased. Sometimes it is difficult to understand them at first indeed, sometimes it is difficult to understand them at all! But that is the magic of art: learning to observe, analyse and discover. Liechtenstein holds plenty of opportunities to train these skills and plenty of art, museums and treasures to discover.

Liechtenstein National Museum

The Liechtenstein National Museum is home to a permanent exhibition showcasing the history and culture of Liechtenstein as well as a number of temporary exhibitions. The Postage Stamp Museum in Vaduz is affiliated to the National Museum and displays artefacts and documents relating to the postage service in Liechtenstein. There is also a local history museum in Schellenberg giving an insight into life in the Principality around 1900.

Liechtenstein Museum of Fine Arts with Hilti Art Foundation

Kunstmuseum Liechtenstein is a museum of modern and contemporary art at the heart of Vaduz. The museum building, opened in 2000, a black cube with a subtly reflective façade, sends out a strong message to the outside world. Inside, spacious exhibition rooms stretch out over two levels, of which the upper one receives daylight through a glass ceiling. The profile of the collection of Kunstmuseum Liechtenstein, which is at the same time the state art collection of the Principality of Liechtenstein, is specifically defined by three-dimensional artworks: sculptures, installations and objects. A particular emphasis is on arte povera and post-minimal art. The collection is showcased in temporary presentations accompanying the major changing exhibitions of international 20th- and 21st-century art.

The new Hilti Art Foundation exhibition building was added to the Kunstmuseum in 2015. This important private collection from Liechtenstein comprises outstanding works of classical modernism and contemporary art. 130 years of art history are thus waiting to be experienced and discovered at Kunstmuseum Liechtenstein.

Treasure Chamber
The Treasure Chamber of the Principality of Liechtenstein in Vaduz, the only museum of its kind in the Alps, focues primarily on exhibits belonging to the Princes of Liechtenstein and other private collectors.

Local and private museums
There are a number of other museums in Liechtenstein. These include the English Building

Art Space in Vaduz, a number of local museums/culture centres and a series of privately run galleries.

National Library
The Liechtenstein National Library is a national library, research library and public library all under one roof. It includes a special collection of publications, recordings and videos from and about Liechtenstein.

Triesen

Sightseeing in Triesen what to see. Complete travel guide
The city is located in a picturesque piedmont area and is considered one of the oldest settlements in the country. During the Middle Ages here lived the nobles. They were building their villas in the beautiful woods and forests of this place, on the tops of hills that feature wonderful views.

The city is divided into an old and a new one; the old part is situated on a hill and this place will be surely very interesting to tourists as here have remained numerous old buildings. Church of St. Gallus built in the 13th century is one of them. Five centuries after its building the church had to be closed because the incorrect location of the basement has created the danger of collapsing walls. The shrine remained abandoned until the middle of the 19th century, when the famous architect Wegmuller has made its full restoration. Today the church is decorated with beautiful paintings and stained glass, and there is also a font of great beauty made of black marble. Only several sculptures have left from the old church.

Another religious landmark is located nearby. This is Chapel of St. Mamertusa. It was founded back in the 9th century; later a tower has been added to it. The main decoration of the church is a triptych made in the Gothic style. During the restoration works in 1967 beautiful murals were discovered on the walls of the church. These murals are created in 14 - 15 centuries.

You should definitely visit St. Mary's Chapel, which was completed in 1654. You can see an image of death on the altar of the chapel. Such an unusual monument reminds visitors of the plague which appeared here in the beginning of the 17th century. Visitors will also find many interesting places and entertainments in the city, including parks, boulevards, restaurants and shops.

Besides seeing the historical sights within the city, guests of Triesen have an opportunity to diversify their rest with walks in picturesque places. In the immediate vicinity of the city is a beautiful Feldkirch natural park where one can observe rare wild animals in their natural habitat. Excellent conditions have been created especially for them. There lives a family of lynx, rare birds and other indigenous forests dwellers. Informative excursions are often held for visitors with children. There are beautiful recreation areas here, as well.

Several prestigious golf centers are located not far from the city. They can be visited during the warm part of the year. Golf courses are arranged in an incredibly beautiful natural area. They're appreciated not only by admirers of the elite sport but also by lovers of nature. You can have a great day together with your family, enjoying the favorite game or strolling the picturesque surroundings.

Triesen lies in a complex hilly terrain. Its territory is conditionally separated into Upper and Lower Town. The Upper Town remains the most interesting part for lovers of tours. It is here, that the main religious attractions and a number of ancient constructions are situated. The historic district is known for the ruins of ancient buildings, created in Roman times. There are many picturesque centuries-old houses in the Old Town. It will be really interesting to walk here.

Triesen will be a perfect holiday destination for lovers of gastronomic tourism. Though the town is quite small, it is full of wonderful national restaurants. They introduce interesting culinary traditions of the region. Local restaurants serve wonderful meat dishes. Almost all of them are very nourishing, so visitors usually share one dish.

Besides gastronomic masterpieces, the region is famous for wonderful wines and liqueurs. You can taste them in national restaurants. There are several specialty stores in the city where one can purchase a bottle of local liqueur or wine as a gift.

Triesen is a great vacation spot for those who are tired of noisy and crowded cities and want to enjoy the distinctive atmosphere of the picturesque region.

The End

Made in the USA
Columbia, SC
13 June 2022